Original title:
Twinkle, Twinkle, Cosmic Verse

Copyright © 2025 Creative Arts Management OÜ
All rights reserved.

Author: George Mercer
ISBN HARDBACK: 978-1-80567-829-8
ISBN PAPERBACK: 978-1-80567-950-9

Celestial Epiphany

In the sky, a giant cheese,
Flies around with greatest ease.
Aliens dance in silly shoes,
Sipping cosmic grape-flavored brews.

Stars twirl like disco balls,
Bouncing off the moonlit walls.
Planets play a game of chase,
Wobbling in their funny space.

Starlit Odyssey

Rockets zoom with honking sounds,
Martians jog on cosmic grounds.
Galaxies throw a pizza night,
With toppings like moon cheese, what a sight!

Asteroids jump in hopscotch games,
While comets wink with silly names.
Shooting stars, they trip and fall,
Making wishes, not for all!

Astral Reflections

In the void where antics reign,
Black holes laugh, they're quite insane.
Saturn's rings are goldfish bowls,
Where funky fish perform their roles.

Jupiter's storms, oh what a scene,
With wind-blown hair, they're quite the queens.
Nebulas dress in polka dots,
Throwing parties with strange robots.

Celestial Symphonies

The sun sings tunes of fresh delight,
While meteors dance through the night.
A symphony of giggles bright,
Each note a star, a pure delight.

Uranus plays a kazoo loud,
While Venus giggles in a cloud.
Together in this cosmic spree,
They make a melody so free.

Echoes of the Night Sky

Stars giggle and dance, oh so bright,
They wink their eyes, causing quite a fright.
Moons are cheeky, playing peek-a-boo,
While comets race past, saying, "Look at you!"

Galaxies swirl, like candy in haze,
Making wishes on sweets, in dizzying ways.
Planets juggling, with flair and with style,
Who knew space had such a comical smile?

Celestial Vignettes

Ghosts of stars whisper silly secrets,
While meteors deliver quirky blessings.
Asteroids laugh, rolling with delight,
As space dust chuckles, floating through the night.

Bubbles of starlight, bursting with cheer,
Singing tunes that only aliens hear.
Strange creatures dance on rings of resplendence,
Making space trips feel like a fun adventure!

Dreaming in Nebulae

In clouds of color, they play hopscotch,
As little stars scribble and doodle a notch.
Whimsical shapes, in a dreamy ballet,
Giggles of gas clouds lead the way!

As dreams float by on their cosmic quest,
Each wish seems to dance; oh, what a jest!
Nebulae sigh, tickled by the light,
Chasing dreams through the velvety night.

Starlight Reverberations

Echoes of laughter ripple in space,
As planets play tag in a whimsical race.
Saturn chuckles, rings spinning with glee,
Uranus snorts, what a sight to see!

Shooting stars pull pranks, make wishes unclear,
As they swirl around like they've had too much beer.
Cosmic confetti of starlight's refrain,
Reminds us that laughter is never in vain!

Cosmic Epiphany

In space where stars like to prance,
The aliens hold a wild dance.
With goofy grins and wobbly feet,
They spin in circles—oh, what a treat!

They claim they've found the perfect snack,
A moon made of cheese, on a cosmic track.
They gobble it up with delight and cheer,
While photon beams burst—not a single tear.

Asteroids roll like bowling balls,
While comets compete in speed trials.
Uranus giggles, its rings are bright,
As it joins in the cosmic night fight!

A black hole hiccupped, what a surprise,
Swallowed a spaceship, but just the fries.
Laughter resonates through the void,
In this universe, joy is enjoyed!

Nebula's Embrace

In colorful clouds where space critters roam,
They knit fuzzy sweaters to keep them at home.
With yarn spun from stardust, every hue,
Galactic knitting is quite the view!

A supernova sneezed, oh what a sight,
Messy particles dancing in flight.
Nebulae giggled, swirling around,
Creating patterns that astound!

Planets hide during this crafty spree,
Dodging stray needles carelessly.
While comets whiz without a care,
Crafting gags with flying hair!

When nebulae gather to share their crafts,
Laughter swirls in celestial drafts.
With each stitch and cosmic embrace,
Life's just a laugh in this vast space!

Celestial Photography

With a camera made of cosmic dust,
Stars strike poses—oh, that's a must!
Galaxies pout with a twinkle in their eye,
While quasar smiles light up the sky.

Nebulas make funny faces at the lens,
Practicing smiles that seem to never end.
Saturn shows off with musical rings,
While meteors act out their dramatic flings!

The Milky Way winks, striking a pose,
Its glittering beauty, everyone knows.
A cosmic photo-bombing crew arrives,
Making memories where pure fun thrives!

In the gallery of the universe bright,
Laughter and wonder dance through the night.
With snapshots of dreams spun into art,
Cosmic silliness reigns in every heart!

Astral Overture

Stars play hide and seek, oh what a sight,
With comets zooming fast, a wild flight.
Galaxies spin like colas uncapped,
While aliens sip tea, all happily strapped.

Planets joke and tumble, laugh out loud,
Jupiter trips on clouds, oh so proud.
Saturn's rings are hula hoops, they tease,
As meteors dance, like they're on wheeze.

Dreams Among the Constellations

Orion's belt is just a string of socks,
Lying around the universe like flocks.
Pisces splashes in what looks like a pool,
While Leo the lion tries to act cool.

The Big Dipper stirs its cosmic stew,
While shooting stars wish they were cats, too!
A cosmic giggle pops through the night,
As galaxies wink with gleeful delight.

Luminary Dance

Dancing lights, oh how they prance,
Creating patterns, a cosmic romance.
Planets swirl in a zany ballet,
Dizzying moves in a space cabaret.

A stellar jig, with a pop and a whirl,
Nebulas twirling, giving a twirl.
With moons on the sidelines, tap shoes on,
Cosmic disco until the break of dawn!

Veils of Light

In the quiet of night, the lights unspool,
A tapestry woven, a celestial jewel.
Stars play peekaboo, hiding and show,
While meteors whizz by, putting on a show.

Veils of color drift, like balloons in the air,
Each hue a chuckle, with a light-hearted flair.
A universe bursting in a giggly display,
As cosmic critters join in the fray!

Space-Time Sonata

Stars do leap and bounce about,
In a vacuum, there's no doubt.
Aliens dance with cosmic cheer,
Wormholes twist, while we all jeer.

Planets wear their silly hats,
Orbiting like silly brats.
Gravity's a playful thing,
Let's just see what chaos brings.

Asteroids spin with wobbly grace,
Comets zoom in a crazy race.
Light-years take their time to play,
In the universe, it's a fun day.

Black holes snicker, sucking light,
Leaving us in our sheer delight.
Cosmic jokes throughout the year,
In this show, there's much to cheer!

Twilight Reverberations

Galaxy giggles fill the air,
As stardust spreads without a care.
Nebulae in colors bright,
Making shadows dance at night.

Aliens trade their silly hats,
While shooting stars do somersaults.
Time bends like a noodle friend,
In this twilight, let's pretend.

Pulsars blink their Morse code thrills,
Echoes of laughter give us chills.
Each planet's mood swings in delight,
As comets play hide and seek each night.

Every meteorite brings a grin,
Cosmic chaos, let the fun begin.
The universe, a silly jest,
In this wonder, we are blessed!

Astral Elysium

In the cosmos, where ducks can fly,
Planets laugh and wink an eye.
Galactic pranks behind the stars,
A game of tag with red guitars.

Asteroids bounce like ball pits
In a dance-off, nobody quits.
Neptune's water balloons do burst,
In this playground, we all must thirst.

Light sabers made of starlight twirl,
Aliens kibitz, twist and whirl.
A supernova's grand display,
Is just a firework that loves to play.

In this realm, all's not so serious,
A light-hearted jest, quite delirious.
Join the fun, let laughter rise,
In the cosmos, joy never lies!

Starstream Reflections

Shooting stars with quirky charms,
In the night, they raise alarms.
Hitch a ride on a comet's tail,
Sailing through a starlit veil.

Jupiter's got a frown today,
While Saturn twirls in a classyway.
Tiny moons juggle with glee,
In this galactic jamboree.

Light-years stretch like fondue cheese,
As we drift on space's breeze.
Cosmic jokes that make us laugh,
An interstellar photograph.

Black holes grin, with mischief in eyes,
Carrying secrets, making us wise.
The cosmos spins its playful song,
Together, we all dance along!

Stellar Whirlwind

In space, the stars all dance and spin,
They trip on comets, giggling with a grin.
Asteroids play tag, zooming past each other,
Making sounds like 'whoosh!'—it's fun, oh brother!

Nebulae swirl, like cotton candy spun,
While planets join in, saying, 'Let's have fun!'
Galaxies laugh, a swirling joker's joke,
As starlight crackles in a cosmic poke.

Night's Tapestry

The moon is laughing, peeking through the trees,
While owls hoot jokes, flapping in the breeze.
Stars are the stitches, glimmering with glee,
Creating a quilt for the night's jubilee.

Meteors dart by, with haircuts so chic,
Making wishes fly, at the speed of sneak.
Each twinkle whispers, 'Hey, you've got a wish!'
While cosmic critters prepare a starfish.

Astral Aurora

Colors burst forth like laughter in the night,
Dancing skies joke with a magical light.
Green and pink giggles paint the air so free,
While aliens wink, sipping glow-in-the-dark tea.

Sparkles and smiles chase away all the gloom,
As constellations joke, lighting up the room.
'Hey look at Ursa! She's tripped on a star!'
Giggles erupt: 'Look how silly we are!'

Shooting Star Whispers

Shooting stars are pranksters, zooming by fast,
Leaving trails of laughter that will always last.
They whisper sweet secrets in the cosmic dance,
While planets shake hands, giving fate a chance.

Wishes get tangled among space's delight,
As galaxies play hopscotch, having a bite.
Stars poke at each other, with humor so bright,
In the vast universe, it's all a delight.

Radiance in Solitude

In space alone, I dance and weave,
Stars giggle softly, oh how I believe.
Asteroids bop, with a clumsy spin,
While comets chuckle, laughing within.

Galaxies swirl like a cosmic show,
Planets play tag, and the moons all glow.
I wave to the dust, so light and spry,
As cosmic confetti drifts from the sky.

Celestial Labyrinth

A maze of stars, oh what a sight,
I lost my way in the cosmic night.
Alien creatures wave from afar,
As I trip on gravity, my own bizarre.

With black holes grinning, they twist and twirl,
I pirouette through, in cosmic whirl.
Space hiccups loudly, a giggle or two,
As I dodge meteorites, saying boo-hoo!

Echoes of Infinity

In the vast void, I shout with glee,
My voice bounces back, oh listen to me!
Echoes of laughter fill up the night,
While planets hum tunes, a joyful flight.

The cosmos chuckles, a chuckle so wide,
As I ride the waves of starlight's tide.
Time does a jig, a funny old prance,
In this infinite place, come join the dance!

Nebulae Song

Colors swirl, a painter's dream,
Nebulae giggle, or so it would seem.
With each puff of gas, they say, "Hey there!"
As I join in their vibrant affair.

Shooting stars wink, like cheeky sprites,
While space dust tickles my funny sights.
In this cosmic choir, we sing along,
The universe chuckles, we're all in this song!

Glittering Echoes

Stars all giggle in the night,
Their dance a blur, a funky sight.
They shout in glee, a cosmic game,
A shimmered chorus, never tame.

Comets zoom with playful grace,
Winking lights in outer space.
Planets spin like tops in jest,
While meteors take a wild rest.

Nebulae wear their colorful hats,
Shooting stars play with the cats.
Galaxies do a silly twirl,
Spreading joy from swirl to swirl.

With every flicker, laugh, and cheer,
Cosmic jokes from far and near.
In the dark, the laughter grows,
A universe that tickles toes.

Radiant Reverie

In the vastness, stars take naps,
Dreaming up their funny maps.
Jupiter wears his biggest grin,
While Saturn spins with rings akin.

Light-years stretch like silly bands,
Stardust sprinkled by cosmic hands.
Wormholes giggle, twisting tight,
Launching dreams into the night.

Shooting stars pass notes in lines,
While black holes snack on lost designs.
Supernovae pop like corn,
As bright eyes wake to a new dawn.

Between the orbs a jest unfolds,
Galactic secrets, laughter told.
Radiant lights bounce off the void,
In cosmic capers, nothing's coyed.

Galactic Lullaby

The universe hums a silly tune,
While asteroids dance around the moon.
Meteor showers throw a fit,
Chasing comets in a goofy skit.

Planets rock in a cosmic cradle,
Satellites spin like a fabled ladle.
Stars are serenading the black expanse,
Inviting the cosmos for a prance.

Quasars sing with all their might,
As galaxies create a soft light.
Cosmic whispers fill the air,
With laughter shared everywhere.

As nebulae swirl, giggles commence,
In this space of vast extravagance.
The lullaby rocks each twinkling friend,
In a dance that never seems to end.

Shimmering Horizons

Horizon glimmers with a grin,
Winking at the stars within.
The sun jokes as it sets down low,
Painting skies with a vibrant show.

constellations play tag at dusk,
In the twilight, they form a busk.
Uranus spins in quirky fashion,
While the night sky gets glittery passion.

Shooting stars sashay in pairs,
Moonbeams chase away all cares.
Celestial bodies laugh and sway,
In playful antics, night turns to day.

As the cosmos paints its grand display,
Laughter echoes in a cosmic ballet.
Horizons shimmer, a joyful spree,
In the universe, wild and free.

Beyond the Horizon

In the sky, a disco ball,
Dancing stars, they have a ball.
Planets play a game of tag,
While comets blast, like a happy rag.

Aliens in tutus prance,
Meteors moonwalk, take a chance.
Galaxies spin, doing the twist,
Cosmic laughter, a starlit mist.

Spaceships zoom, they take a trip,
On a cosmic roller-skate flip.
Asteroids join in for the cheer,
Cosmic fun, there's nothing to fear!

From afar, they giggle and peek,
Shooting stars play hide and seek.
Beyond the horizon, what a sight,
A universe filled with pure delight!

Celestial Storytelling

Once upon a time on a moon,
Sat a cat that hummed a tune.
Stars spun tales of cosmic glee,
Of a fish who wanted to be free.

He floated on a cosmic wave,
Claiming worlds, oh so brave!
Jupiter laughed, what a jest,
That fish was truly the very best!

A dog joined in, chasing a kite,
Made of stardust, oh what a sight!
Together they flew far and wide,
With cosmic tales, as their guide.

In the end, they shared a feast,
Of meteor pies, a galactic beast.
So gather 'round, lend me your ear,
For celestial stories, we hold dear!

Shimmering Horizons

On shimmering waves of light,
Danced a snail in a spacesuit, quite right!
Flashing neon, silly and bold,
In cosmic waters, treasures unfold.

Stars giggle, on waves they ride,
Fish in sunglasses, with cosmic pride.
Aliens toss glitter in the air,
Laughing together without a care.

Rockets whiz past, making a scene,
While space bunnies jump in between.
A fairytale sprinkles across the sky,
With a wink and a nod, they all fly high.

Horizons shimmering with delight,
In a universe painted bright.
Let's dive deeper into the fun,
For cosmic laughter has just begun!

Lights in the Abyss

In the dark, a glow so bright,
Frogs in spacesuits, what a sight!
Jumping through black holes with glee,
They croak their jokes, full of esprit.

A jellyfish in a tutu sways,
Twinkling lights in whimsical ways.
Asteroids chuckle, rolling around,
In this abyss, joy can be found.

Octopuses twirl with a touch of grace,
Dancing amidst stars in this place.
Laughter echoes through cosmic space,
As strange little critters find their place.

So if you wander to the night,
Watch for the critters, shining bright.
In the abyss, they make their cheer,
With glowing lights, they'll draw you near!

Celestial Canvas

Stars are winking from afar,
Painting dreams on a milk jar.
Planets dance in silly shoes,
Making cosmic silly news.

Comets race with ice cream cones,
While aliens launch funky groans.
The sun tries on a goofy grin,
As moonbeams splash a little spin.

Radiant Silhouettes

In the sky, a cat takes flight,
Chasing shadows in the night.
Meteors play hide and seek,
Launching jokes with every peak.

Rocket ships that giggle loud,
Making their way through the cloud.
Stars are dressed in polka dots,
In a universe full of spots.

Interstellar Musing

Why does Saturn wear a ring?
To impress a cosmic king!
Mars tells jokes that make stars chuckle,
While asteroids dance and shuffle.

Uranus wears a funny hat,
Bouncing with a cosmic cat.
In this dance, we all partake,
Laughing at the cosmic wake.

Velvet Nightfall

As night falls in a fuzzy blur,
The stars all start to giggle and stir.
Constellations form a band,
Playing tunes across the land.

Planets spin in silly sways,
Caught up in the night's wild plays.
The moon tries out its stand-up set,
In a cosmic circus, no regret!

Starlit Whispers

A star fell down and bumped my toe,
Now I dance like a disco show.
It giggled bright, then took a flight,
Claiming it's just too hot for night.

I asked a comet for some tips,
On how to make the best of slips.
It winked at me with a fiery beard,
And said, "Just laugh if you get feared!"

The moon gave me a silly grin,
Said, "Get ready, let the fun begin!"
With martians sharing jokes and cheer,
We'll laugh so hard the stars will hear!

So if you spot a star up high,
Just remember, it might not be shy,
It may be laughing at our plight,
Shooting across the skies in delight.

Celestial Dance

In the sky, the planets spin,
Making faces, trying to begin.
The sun said, "Hey, don't take that stance!"
And gave the moon a little chance.

A few asteroids tried to slide,
But ended up in a cosmic ride.
They spun around, and lost their way,
Shouting, "We're stars! Hip-hip-hooray!"

A black hole laughed, a comical sight,
Said, "Come on down, it's a fun fright!"
With stardust sprinkled all around,
We twirled and giggled without a sound.

And as we danced on meteoric beams,
Dreaming up the silliest schemes,
The universe winked, a ripe joke told,
The secrets of space are never old.

Luminous Dreams

In dreams where light bulbs seem to glow,
I chased a shooting star, oh so slow.
It turned to say, with a playful wink,
"Don't rush, dear friend, let's have a drink!"

The Milky Way threw a surprise bash,
With martini moons and a cosmic splash.
Aliens brought the snacks and cheese,
While stars refueled with cosmic breeze.

I asked a nebula for a dance,
It swirled around, in a colorful trance.
Together we laughed at cosmic tales,
As rockets whizzed like merry gales.

Now I float in a galaxy rich,
Where every star has a funny pitch.
The skies may shimmer, but don't you fret,
It's laughter we'll have, you can bet!

Night's Serenade

The crickets serenade the night,
While planets giggle, oh what a sight!
The owls hoot laughs in syncopated beats,
While comets drop in for tasty treats.

A galaxy's worth of silly songs,
A chorus of star-folk that's never wrong.
They sing about socks that get lost in space,
And the way Earth's got that funny face.

The dark brings jokes that last till dawn,
In this cosmic comedy, I'll respond.
With space raccoons in a zany caper,
And moonlit giggles that sweetly taper.

So grab your friends, and join the cheer,
In a stellar show, there's nothing to fear.
Just follow the laughs, let the stars lead on,
With silliness shining until the night's gone!

Cosmic Serenade

In the night, stars play chess,
Each one thinks it's the best.
Comets dance with silly glee,
While asteroids sip herbal tea.

Galaxies spin in a whirl,
Planets wear their finest pearl.
Aliens laugh, they do cartwheels,
In space, they share their meals.

Black holes yawn, take a break,
Saying, "Oops! Did we make a mistake?"
Nebulas blend colors so bright,
This cosmic party lasts all night!

With a wink and a cosmic shout,
Stars joke about the lack of doubt.
Laughter echoes, a jovial sound,
In the universe, fun's abound!

Luminous Tides

Moonbeams bounce on wavy seas,
Fish sing songs, asking for cheese.
With giggles, the tides start to roll,
As seaweed dances, a silly shoal.

Stars play tag with the shimmering waves,
Each trying to outshine, like cosmic knaves.
Crabs crack jokes on the sandy shore,
While the octopus plans a galactic tour.

Seashells whisper secrets in jest,
"Who's the fastest? Let's put it to test!"
Dolphins flip, sporting their shades,
In this fun, no one fades!

With bright glow from the moonlit skies,
The ocean laughs, what a surprise!
Each wave has its own little rhyme,
In luminous tides, oh what a time!

Stellar Rhapsody

Stars compose a funky tune,
They strum the sighing light of noon.
Shooting stars make a silly fuss,
As meteors are late to their bus.

Galactic squirrels gather round,
Chasing comets that swirl and bound.
Rockets zoom, purring with glee,
As space cats chase them with jubilee.

Each planet hums a different beat,
While sunflowers sway on solar heat.
Asteroids toss a cosmic ball,
In this rhapsody, they have a ball!

With giggles rising from the void,
Laughter echoes, joy unalloyed.
The universe smiles, wants more fun,
In stellar rhapsody, we all run!

Radiant Reflections

Mirrors float in the starry sky,
Winking at planets that pass by.
A nebula giggles, flicks a light,
While black holes munch on cosmic bite.

Supernovae throw a glow,
While space chickens begin to crow.
Their feathers sparkle, what a sight,
Cooking up stars for a midnight bite.

"Why is space so full of cheer?"
With each twinkle, spirits near.
Creatures chat about the dark,
Setting off a cosmic spark!

In these reflections, we find the fun,
Where laughter echoes, never done.
From every corner of the night,
Radiant joy takes its flight!

Celestial Nocturne

In a galaxy far, far away,
Planets dance and spin, hooray!
A cow jumped over the moon's cheese,
While aliens giggle with glee.

Shooting stars wear silly hats,
Comets teasing little cats.
The sun just rolled its eyes and yawned,
As night's pranks swiftly dawned.

Moonbeams slip on banana peels,
Starry laughs are what it feels.
Galactic jesters play their games,
While we all forget our names.

So if you peek at night, be sure,
To hear the tales, they'll allure.
Cosmic giggles fill the air,
In the night's enchanted fair.

Starfire Chronicles

Once in the sky, a star wore socks,
Dancing around like paradox.
The universe, full of funny sights,
With comets that throw wild space fights.

The planets roll their eyes and snicker,
As black holes hide their secrets quicker.
Asteroids play peek-a-boo,
While stardust makes a candy stew.

Jupiter eats at a cosmic diner,
Mars orders fries, oh, could it be finer?
Each planet with a quirky flair,
Bringing joy to the cosmic air.

When meteors race for the fun of it,
The Milky Way laughs, never does sit.
In the void, where laughter brews,
Cosmic tales become nightly news.

Aurora's Embrace

In the northern skies, a dance unfolds,
Colors swirl like stories told.
An aurora giggles and spins so bright,
Chasing the shadows of stars at night.

With every flash, a wink and grin,
The night sky plays, it's ready to win.
Clouds wear pajamas, fluffy and round,
While stars play hide and seek around.

Oh, the comets make faces, left and right,
Chasing space dreams, what a silly sight!
Planets share jokes, laughter galore,
As they tumble through the cosmic floor.

So as you gaze at the flick'ring spark,
Remember the fun in the cosmic dark.
For every shimmer and shine you see,
Is a cosmic giggle, wild and free.

Infinite Illumination

Among the stars, a radish flew,
Chasing its dream—a cosmic stew!
Galaxies swirl with jellybeans,
While black holes hide their movie scenes.

The sun sips tea on a solar chair,
Waves to the moon, "Join me, if you dare!"
Meteor showers drop candy bars,
As Saturn spins with its ring of stars.

Aliens toast with chocolate milk,
As cosmic dust flows soft as silk.
Stars wear glasses, smart and chic,
Giggling softly, every week.

So explore the night with a smile so wide,
For it's a carnival where dreams abide.
In the heavenly show where laughter's free,
All the cosmos sings joyfully.

Cosmic Symphony

In the sky, a dance begins,
Stars play notes on violins.
The moon dips low, starts to prance,
While comets spin in cosmic dance.

Planets wear their snazzy hats,
Jupiter skips while Saturn chats.
Mars is busy baking pies,
While Venus juggles bouncing flies.

Asteroids join in the beat,
With meteors tapping their feet.
It's a party up above,
A galactic tale of love.

So grab your friends, let's take flight,
To join this stellar, starry night.
With laughter echoing so bright,
We sway beneath the cosmic light.

Enigmatic Skies

In hues of blue, the clouds do laugh,
While sunbeams draw a silly graph.
Aliens flip through interstellar books,
Drawing faces with funny looks.

The Milky Way plays peek-a-boo,
Popping out with stars, just for you.
They wink and giggle, oh what fun,
As shooting stars are on the run.

A UFO does cartwheels bright,
While space cows soar into the night.
Galactic squirrels munch on cheese,
Making merry with cosmic ease.

So let your dreams take off with glee,
In these mysterious skies, come see.
A universe filled with charm and cheer,
With every giggle that we hear.

Chasing Stardust

With a net in hand, I chase the light,
Hopping through the galaxy bright.
Stardust giggles, slips away,
Like slippery fish, they bounce and play.

I trip on Saturn's shiny rings,
Giggling hard at the joy it brings.
Chasing orbs that zig and zag,
Joking with the stars, oh what a drag!

Comets tease with swift ballet,
While I puff, 'Hey, not today!'
They whirl and twirl, moonwalk their way,
Leaving me to gasp and sway.

But in the chase, I find my groove,
With every hop, my spirit moves.
What cosmic laughter fills the night,
As I chase dreams in endless flight.

Symphony of Light

The stars take stage for a grand show,
With lasers dancing, stealing the glow.
Galaxies swirl in wacky turns,
While quarks and leptons jive and churn.

A sunbeam sings a snazzy tune,
While shadows bob like a balloon.
Light travels fast, but it trips on air,
Knocking over a spacetime chair.

The pulsars beep a rhythmic beat,
While bright nebulae tap their feet.
A rhythm so goofy, it can't be missed,
A cosmic fiesta with an alien twist.

So let's join in this vibrant jam,
Where even black holes strum a klam.
Under the lights, we dance and sway,
In this symphony that leads the way.

Infinite Glimmers

Stars like popcorn in the sky,
Popping with laughter, oh so spry.
Jupiter's dancing, doing the twist,
While Mars just chuckles, can't resist.

Aliens giggle, whizzing by,
Trading jokes on their way to fly.
A comet sneezes, a funny sight,
Leaving trails of sparkles bright.

The moon cracks jokes with starlit friends,
While cosmic winds carry giggle trends.
In this vastness, laughter swirls,
Like a cosmic party with space-age pearls.

So when you gaze up at the night,
Remember the stars are laughing bright.
Join in the fun, let your heart soar,
In this universe, there's always more!

Night's Palette

The sky's a painter with a brush,
Splatters of laughter in a cosmic hush.
Moonbeams tickle, colors collide,
Swirling giggles from galaxies wide.

Comets whiz by, slipping on ice,
While Saturn's rings spin, oh so nice.
Each star a wink, each planet a grin,
In this grand canvas, all can win.

Auroras dance, like jelly on toast,
While stardust sparkles, it loves the most.
Nebulas giggle in hues so bright,
Painting the fabric of endless night.

Join the fun, don your cosmic hat,
With laughter stitched in the sky, imagine that!
As night unfolds its wacky delight,
Let's laugh with the stars till morning light!

Galactic Lullaby

Hush now, little stars, don't fall too fast,
In this galaxy, the fun's a blast!
The Milky Way sings a silly tune,
With bouncing asteroids that sway to the moon.

Planets play tag in a jovial race,
Mars gives a wink, "I'm winning this space!"
Neptune giggles, splashing about,
While the sun warms up, giving a shout.

In this lullaby of cosmic fun,
Even black holes love to run.
With stardust pillows and comet sheets,
Snuggle up tight, there's laughter in fleets.

So close your eyes, let dreams take flight,
In this universe, everything's light.
As galaxies twirl in the softest sway,
Sleep tight, little dreamers, till the break of day!

Ethereal Glimpse

In the cosmic soup, a noodle that bends,
Galaxies giggle, oh how time spins!
Spaghetti stars in an interstellar plate,
Eating stardust, it can't wait!

A flying fish swims in a sea of light,
Telling tales of its magical flight.
With laughter echoing among the cliffs,
As planets gather for cosmic riffs.

"Hey, is that an asteroid, or just a rock?"
Planetary friends burst into shock!
Shooting stars zoom, making a jest,
In this park of the universe, they're truly blessed.

So take a peek at this whimsical scene,
Where laughter flutter in the gaps between.
With each playful wink, a sparkle you'll find,
A joyful reminder we're all intertwined!

Moonbeam Soliloquy

Oh moonbeam, you silly bright light,
Dance on my nose, that's quite a sight!
Were you raised by stars in the night?
Or just a joke from the sky, polite?

Bouncing around like a playful pup,
Sipping stardust from an empty cup.
Will you share a laugh, or just erupt?
Your glow is a gag, that lifts me up!

Did you ever stumble on a comet?
Or fall asleep in a giant bonnet?
You light up the world, but wait—you've won it!
A heavenly laugh, no one can shun it!

Moonbeam, oh friend, with your glowing spree,
Come shine on our jokes, just you and me!
In this cosmic circus, we feel so free,
Forever your fan, in giggles we'll be!

Cosmic Harmonies

In the galaxy's band, where quarks play soft,
Planets rehearse, while comets scoff.
What a catchy tune, the stars lift off,
Singing space songs from a cosmic trough!

A black hole drummer, with a mighty beat,
Pulling all sound to a fun retreat.
While Saturn's rings keep the rhythm sweet,
Playing melodies that none can defeat!

Shooting stars are backup, oh what a flair,
Winking at us with sparkles to share.
In this cosmic concert, we dance in air,
While planets giggle without a care!

So grab your space boots, let's strut and sway,
Join in this jam, come on, what do you say?
With laughter and joy, come out and play,
In cosmic harmonies, we'll laugh all day!

Nebula's Secrets

What secrets reside in a nebula's fold?
Is there gossip of stars that we've yet to be told?
With colors so bright, they shimmer and scold,
Are they whispering tales of the universe bold?

I peek through the haze, with a wink and a grin,
Are you hiding a planet, or a grumpy old fin?
A cosmic magician, just pulling me in,
Spilling silly stories of where to begin!

Fluffy and fuzzy, like cotton in air,
Are these clouds of space laughing, unaware?
With secrets of joy, they swirl without care,
Telling the cosmos, "There's fun everywhere!"

So let's ponder deep as the stardust whirls,
And giggle at space as it twirls and twirls.
With cosmic shenanigans, let laughter unfurl,
In the nebula's secrets, let's dance and twirl!

Ethereal Twilight

In twilight's embrace, where shadows do play,
The stars start to chuckle, they brighten the way.
With giggles from Venus, what fun to convey,
While Jupiter jests that night's just a ballet!

The sun's taking naps, in a cozy retreat,
While galaxies waltz, oh so light on their feet.
Planets trade jokes, all good-natured and sweet,
As they spin their wild tales, a whimsical feat!

Fleeting comets zoom, with a whoosh and a grin,
Saying "Catch me if you can!" as they zoom in.
We'll race with the meteors, who's losing or win?
In this twilight dance, let the fun begin!

So lift up your spirits, let laughter ignite,
In the magic of dusk, where the dark meets the light.
With starlit tomfoolery, the heavens delight,
Ethereal twilight, where joy takes its flight!

Aurora's Prism

In a sky that plays with glitz,
Stars wear hats, what a great blitz!
Dancing lights, all in a row,
They've got moves, don't you know?

Green and pink, a giddy flair,
Cosmic giggles fill the air!
Who knew space had this much fun?
Swirling colors, here they run!

Gravity's a silly chap,
Trying hard to mind the map.
While planets roll like bowling balls,
In this dance, nobody falls!

So let your heart lighten the probe,
As we twirl in this bright globe.
Where stars play silly hide and seek,
Join the cosmic laugh, so unique!

Celestial Baubles

Look up high, the sky's a show,
Bouncing beads in cosmic flow.
A comet sneezes, what a blast!
Space is lively, having a laugh!

Stars wear sunglasses, what a sight,
Winking down, oh what a night!
Each tiny dot has tales to share,
Of far-off worlds and silly air!

Planets giggle, rolling round,
On orbits where fun is found.
Jupiter's got a booming voice,
Singing tunes that make us rejoice!

So raise your gaze and take a ride,
In this cosmic joke, let's glide.
Our laughter echoes through the dark,
A shining world, a flickered spark!

Dazzling Constellations

Orion's belt has lost its pants,
He's moonwalking, taking his chance!
The Big Dipper's making soup,
A celestial festive loop!

The Little Bear has found a friend,
A rubber duck, they start to blend.
Stars are drawing funny faces,
Creating cosmic, silly places!

Perseus rides a shooting star,
He thinks it's just a funky car!
And Cassiopeia's doing spins,
While Venus laughs and chugs her sins!

Let's toast to stars, those jolly fools,
Who play around like cosmic schools.
With every glance, their fun we borrow,
Bring on the stars, let's laugh 'til tomorrow!

Cosmic Drift

On this ship of cosmic glee,
Sailing through infinity!
Asteroids play hopscotch bright,
In this zany, starry light.

Black holes jest, they swirl and twirl,
Sucking up a cosmic pearl!
While comets race with silly grace,
In the great galactic space!

Planets wink with cheeky grins,
Spinning tales of cosmic twins.
Each star has quirks, a little flair,
Let's laugh and dance without a care!

So drift along in spacey charm,
Find laughter's warmth, it's such a balm.
The universe is rich with cheer,
A funny place to explore, my dear!

Galaxy's Gaze

In the void, a star can wink,
A cosmic jester, don't you think?
Planets dance, they spin and twirl,
Making faces, giving a whirl.

Comets zoom with tails so bright,
Like cosmic dogs in endless flight.
Asteroids play cosmic hide and seek,
Who's the fastest? Sneaky and sleek!

Nebulas puff like colorful clowns,
While black holes swirl with ominous frowns.
Galaxies craft their own funny tales,
With giggles echoing through the scales.

Space is wild, a circus in flight,
Stars on stilts, what a sight!
So let's laugh beneath the night sky,
As we join the universe's sly high-five!

Lightplay in the Dark

In shadows deep, a light sneaks out,
Playing peek-a-boo with a shout.
Each flicker bursts with silly cheer,
While galaxies giggle, can you hear?

Neon moons wear jazzy shoes,
Dancing round in cosmic blues.
Shooting stars take leaps and bounds,
With laughter ringing all around.

Space clouds puff and puff away,
Sneaky whispers in the Milky Way.
Lightsabers clash, oh, what a mess,
As aliens compete in a mini dress.

Gravity's pulling pranks with flair,
Spinning 'round like it just don't care.
So throw your wishes, let them spark,
Join the fun in this cosmic park!

Infinite Stargaze

Stars align in a playful brawl,
Who's the shiniest of them all?
Galaxies giggle, swaying wide,
As stardust tickles, can't decide!

Planets wear hats, some twisty, some neat,
While moons juggle their cheese for a treat.
Cosmic pals share secret jokes,
As meteors race in silly cloaks.

Wormholes spin tales of cosmic lore,
With breakout shows and encore galore.
Slipping through time like it's a game,
Space-time giggles, who's to blame?

So gaze up high, let your heart race,
For the sky's a carnival, a wild place!
With laughter echoing through the space,
Join the fun, there's joy to embrace!

Solar Serenities

In sunbeams, giggles rise,
Bouncing off of starlit skies.
Solar flares do silly jigs,
As planets pop like bouncing pigs.

Light years away, they play charades,
One star shines, but the other fades.
Eclipses hide, then give a shout,
Surprise parties on the cosmic route!

Solar winds are ticklish and zany,
As comets retrieve their rocks and grainy.
Each flash ignites a funny scheme,
In this universe, a cosmic dream!

So dance among the twinkling lights,
With cosmic laughter soaring heights.
For in this galactic serenade,
We find the joy that never fades!

Beyond the Event Horizon

In space where the rules start to bend,
A sock thief waits, your favorite friend.
He steals all the pairs, then dances with glee,
And laughs at the chaos, oh what a spree!

A black hole grins, a mischievous sight,
It swallows your snacks, now isn't that bright?
With a wink and a nudge, it pulls you near,
'I'll keep your chips safe,' it says with a cheer!

Supernovae pop like a cosmic surprise,
Stars want to party, they light up the skies.
Twinkling umbrellas emerge from the dust,
While aliens sip tea and giggle, they must!

In the galaxy's heart, laughter has no end,
While planets are spinning, the comets descend.
It's a riot up here, with space much to tease,
So join in the fun, just float with the breeze!

Ethereal Lightwaves

A light wave stumbles, trips on a star,
It wiggles and jiggled, traveling far.
Photons wear shades, looking suave in the night,
While gravity's pulling, they dance out of sight!

In the depths of a nebula, jokes come alive,
With clouds full of puns, the laughter will thrive.
'Why did the comet bring a friend to the show?
Because a shooting star's not fun on its own!'

Asteroids roll like they've lost their way,
Bouncing through space like kids at a play.
In an orbit of laughter, they crack jokes that excite,
As stardust giggles in the shimmering light!

In this topsy-turvy, zany cosmic dance,
All celestial bodies are up for a chance.
To whirl with delight, yelling 'Whee!' with the sky,
As galaxies whirl, in a grand cosmic tie!

Cosmic Fables

Once there was a star with a laugh so loud,
It tickled the planets and roused a crowd.
While Jupiter boogied with Saturn in tow,
Mars just rolled over, 'Let's steal the show!'

Uranus wore glasses, looked smart and refined,
But tripped on a moon, oh my, what a find!
With rings full of giggles, they spun in delight,
Making jokes about meteors falling from sight!

In the vast cosmic library, tales wax and wane,
With comets dictating, they're never mundane.
'Why did the star blush?' one asked with a grin,
'Because it saw the black hole take a spin!'

Each night brings a story, a laugh, and a cheer,
As bubbles of light frolic, drawing near.
So gather your stardust, set dreams in the air,
For the cosmos tells jokes, beyond all compare!

Nightfall Ballet

The moon takes a bow, and the stars join in,
With a pirouette here, and a spin with a grin.
Galactic dancers swirl in a jest,
While Saturn leads off, looking quite dressed!

Comets in tutus, they glide down the lane,
They slip and they slide, yet never complain.
While space-time wobbles, a silly ballet,
As planets all cheer, 'Hooray for this play!'

Constellations giggle, they can't keep it straight,
As they fumble for names, oh what a fate!
'Is that a bear or a ladle up there?'
Laughter erupts as the stars pull a dare!

So come join the fun, beneath the bright skies,
With a wink and a whirl, let imagination rise.
In this playful night, we all find a role,
As we dance through the cosmos, the merriment whole!

Star-Kissed Verses

A little star wearing shades,
Chasing planets in parades.
Winking down from lofty heights,
Making friends with silly flights.

Comets tailing lost balloons,
Juggling moons like giant spoons.
Galaxies in dance so grand,
Shaking hands with any band.

Shooting stars take coffee breaks,
Sharing jokes with cosmic flakes.
Laughing at their sparkly fates,
Setting up interstellar dates.

A starry night, a comic show,
With cosmic gags that steal the glow.
Each laughter echoing through space,
A universe of funny grace.

Stellar Reverie

Stars play hide and seek in glee,
While black holes sip their cosmic tea.
Meteor showers throw confetti,
In space, it's always big and petty.

Gravity pulling pranks on light,
Making orbits spin just right.
Planets dance in quirky ways,
With space-time tangled in a maze.

Aliens laugh at Earth's grand plan,
Bouncing 'round like a rubber band.
With their antennas all aglow,
They're OH-SO-Silly, don't you know?

Asteroids toss a cosmic pie,
While aliens giggle as they fly.
In this vast galactic spree,
Who knew space could be so free?

Illuminated Solstice

The sun wearing a party hat,
While planets dance and do a splat.
Stars don't stop at silly things,
They juggle with the dream of kings.

In the ring of cosmic cheer,
Planets sing without a fear.
"Let's throw a solar disco night!"
As asteroids join in the light.

Black holes bouncing like a ball,
Grinning wide and having a ball.
Supernovae bursting with flair,
While space-time plays musical chairs.

Meteorites drop silly beats,
As comets strut on cosmic streets.
A celebration cosmic style,
Bringing laughter across the miles.

Luminary Lull

Stars whisper secrets in the dark,
While comets build a playground park.
Wormholes tease with playful spins,
Making spacetime do its wins.

Gravitational waves do the twist,
As dancing moons swing with a mist.
Galactic fairies paint the skies,
With joy that makes us laugh and rise.

Meteorites tell tales so grand,
Of cosmic ice cream in their hand.
And stardust giggles on its way,
Launching dreams where wishes play.

Galaxies gaze with sparkling eyes,
Joking with the sun that never dies.
In this humor-filled, luminous night,
Every blink brings pure delight.

Celestial Choreography

In the night sky, stars do prance,
Dancing in a stellar chance.
Planets spin like tops, oh dear,
Shining bright, but drinking beer!

Comets zoom with wagging tails,
Wishing on them surely fails.
Aliens peek through telescope,
Planning parties—oh, what a trope!

Moon's a lazy, cheese-filled ball,
Who invited him to this ball?
Galaxies flaunt their glitter and glow,
Strutting down the cosmic show!

So let's toast to skies so dark,
With a wink and a little spark.
Stars are silly, that much is true,
Spreading giggles, just for you!

Distant Flickers

In the depths of space, a light does wink,
A star with a smile—did you think?
It's trying to make the moon laugh,
But moon's too busy with its own craft.

A rainbow comet's straying here,
Catching stardust, sipping beer.
Saturn's rings bling bright at night,
Sparkling like a disco's light!

Beyond our world, in cosmic fun,
Jupiter's throwing a quirky pun.
His storms are just a wrestling match,
With lightning moves, what a catchy catch!

So look above and spot the fun,
The universe glows—everyone's spun!
Through laughter and light, it's plain to see,
Space is a joke; just let it be!

Nocturnal Hymn

In the velvet dark, a chorus sings,
Crickets join in, flapping wings.
The owl hoots a tune so neat,
While stars clap paws on furry feet.

A raccoon steals stardust snacks,
Galactic treats from cosmic packs.
He nibbles freely on moonlight pie,
With candy comets rolling by.

Shooting stars make silly sounds,
As laughter ripples through the bounds.
The night is a stage, a grand parade,
Where glowworms gather, unafraid.

So let your worries drift away,
In this celestial cabaret.
Under cosmic laughter, twinkling bright,
The night is ours, pure delight!

Starry Aspirations

Stars have dreams, as odd as they sound,
Wishing on turtles that roam around.
They want to dance on Mars's red,
And paint the sky with colors spread.

One star wants to be in a movie show,
Saying, "Catch me if you can—it's a glow!"
Another is building a rocket ship,
Hoping for an interstellar trip.

A constellation holds an art degree,
Sketching comets with wild glee.
They dream to twirl in a solar ballet,
Making space the stage of play!

So marvel at those shining beams,
In the universe, chasing dreams.
If stars are funny and oh so bright,
Join their antics in the night!

Cosmic Wonderings

Stars wink from afar, oh so bright,
Planets spinning in playful flight.
Aliens sipping tea on the moon,
Joking about Earth's silly tunes.

Comets rush by, tails in a swish,
Meteorites zapping like a fish.
Galaxies twirl in a dizzy dance,
Space is the place for a cosmic prance.

Black holes yawning, what a sight,
Sucking in light with all their might.
Cosmic dust bunnies float in space,
Chasing each other in a fun race.

Gravity giggles, pulling us down,
While we wear our silliest crown.
Floating like balloons in this vast playground,
The universe laughs, what a joyful sound!

Phosphorescent Dreams

In the night, glowworms start to sing,
While the stars join in, doing their thing.
Shooting stars race for a bite to eat,
Nibbling on moonbeams, what a treat!

Dreams take flight on a comet's tail,
Riding the winds of a cosmic gale.
Wishing on lights that flicker and flare,
While rubber ducks float in lunar air.

Aliens dressed in pajamas and socks,
Share their snacks of interstellar rocks.
They giggle and play in the starry haze,
Chasing their tails in a glittering maze.

As night unfolds with a twinkling grace,
Cosmic dreams bring a smile to each face.
Join the party where laughter is free,
In phosphorescent moments, just you and me!

Night's Embrace

The moon tells tales of days gone by,
While owls up high catch a snoozy sigh.
Crickets chirp in a silly choir,
As fireflies dance, setting night afire.

Dreamboats sail on stardust streams,
While kittens leap in the land of dreams.
Mice with goggles fly through the night,
Steering their ships, oh what a sight!

Sassy stars wink, giving little kicks,
As the planets join in with cosmic tricks.
The universe bustles with giggles and glee,
While we cuddle close, just you and me.

In night's embrace, let laughter unfold,
As stories of space come brightly retold.
With silly constellations to keep us warm,
The cosmos whispers, oh what a charm!

Celestial Conversations

Planets gossip about Earth's news,
Saying, "Have you seen their funny shoes?"
Stars spill secrets, winking with cheer,
While meteors boast of their speedy career.

Galaxies swirl with a cosmic cheer,
Chatting with comets that zoom ever near.
"Can you believe what's happening down there?"
"Are they still wearing those wild hairstyles?" they declare.

Moonbeams stretch like happy cats,
As they tickle the sun, and that's that.
Satellites joke about their long waits,
Saying, "At least we don't have to meet dates!"

In the universe's fun-filled spree,
Every star shines with a chuckle, you see.
Join the laughter, it's cosmic delight,
In celestial conversations, all through the night!

Cosmic Crescendo

In a rocket made of cheese,
Zooming past a cosmic sneeze,
Stars all giggle, what a sight,
Asteroids dance, oh what a night!

Galaxies do the funky dance,
Comets twirl in neon pants,
Planets play a game of tag,
While sunbeams wear a shiny rag.

Uranus jokes, it's quite the tease,
Making sure no one's at ease,
Jupiter laughs, with winds a-blow,
While Saturn spins in disco glow.

Oh, cosmic friends, come join the fun,
In this vastness, we are one,
With stardust dreams and silly schemes,
The universe bursts at the seams!

Dark Matter Dreams

In the shadows where stars confide,
Dark matter hides, but who's inside?
Whispers echo through space so wide,
What if black holes just like to glide?

Asteroids with sunglasses on,
Strut around till the break of dawn,
They snack on starlight, oh so bright,
Chirping tunes that feel just right.

Nebulae in colors so bold,
Tell tall tales of wonders untold,
While cosmic kittens chase moonbeams,
And play with galaxies in their dreams.

When gravity pulls, and time stands still,
Whirling through the cosmic thrill,
In the laughter of the universe's scheme,
We find ourselves in dark matter dreams.

Heavenly Glimmers

In a galaxy of jellybeans,
Shooting stars make silly scenes,
With gummy bears that zip and zoom,
Creating chaos in their room.

Celestial cupcakes float around,
With sprinkles like stardust on the ground,
Each bite a taste of cosmic cheer,
Gravity says, 'Float a little near!'

Silly aliens in top hats sway,
Twirling comets in a ballet,
While supernovae pop their confetti,
And stars giggle, oh so ready!

In this banquet of heavenly glimmers,
Where laughter flows as the light shimmers,
We dance among the cosmic treats,
With joyful hearts and tasty beats!

Starry Tranquility

Under a sky of cookie dough,
Stars play hide and seek, they glow,
While meteors munch on chocolate bars,
And moonlight sparkles in our jars.

Galaxies whisper secret rhymes,
As planets giggle in playful times,
They spin around like tops in glee,
Making the comets laugh so free.

Shooting stars wear party hats,
While space cats lounge on cosmic mats,
In the stillness of the night,
Joy dances in the starlit sight.

Oh, starry skies of tranquil highs,
With chuckles wrapped in twinkling ties,
We float along this merry spree,
In the vastness, we find glee!

www.ingramcontent.com/pod-product-compliance
Lightning Source LLC
Chambersburg PA
CBHW051634160426
43209CB00004B/647